Frank Lloyd Wright

MASTERWORKS
A BOOK OF POSTCARDS

Pomegranate
SAN FRANCISCO

Pomegranate Communications, Inc.
Box 6099
Rohnert Park, CA 94927
www.pomegranate.com

Pomegranate Europe Ltd.
Fullbridge House, Fullbridge
Maldon, Essex CM9 4LE
England

ISBN 0-7649-0517-1
Pomegranate Catalog No. A548

© 1999 The Frank Lloyd Wright Foundation
Taliesin West, Scottsdale, Arizona. All rights reserved

Pomegranate publishes books of
postcards on a wide range of subjects.
Please write to the publisher for more information.

Designed by Harrah Argentine
Printed in Korea
07 06 05 04 03 02 01 00 99   10 9 8 7 6 5 4 3 2

To facilitate detachment of the postcards from this book, fold each card along its perforation line before tearing.

Frank Lloyd Wright profoundly changed the art of architecture. In the course of a career that lasted into seven decades, he boldly challenged new materials and technologies, redefining space and creating in the process hundreds of buildings of astonishing imagination and beauty.

Wright loved to draw, and his skill is legendary. "To this day I love to hold a handful of many colored pencils and open my hand to see them lying upon my palm, in the light," he wrote at the age of sixty-one. Draftsmen and apprentices helped to transform his ideas into presentation and working drawings, but Wright's genius energizes each one.

■ MASTERWORKS

Solomon R. Guggenheim Museum
New York, New York, 1943–1959
Perspective. Tempera on black illustration board, 27 x 40 in.
4305.062

Pomegranate BOX 6099 ROHNERT PARK CA 94927

FRANK LLOYD WRIGHT® COLLECTION © THE FRANK LLOYD WRIGHT FOUNDATION TALIESIN WEST, SCOTTSDALE, ARIZONA. ALL RIGHTS RESERVED

■ MASTERWORKS

Isidore Heller House
Chicago, Illinois, 1897
Perspective. Pencil, ink, and ink wash on paper, 9 x 20¼ in.
9606.007

Pomegranate   BOX 6099   ROHNERT PARK   CA 94927

FRANK LLOYD WRIGHT® COLLECTION   © THE FRANK LLOYD WRIGHT FOUNDATION   TALIESIN WEST, SCOTTSDALE, ARIZONA. ALL RIGHTS RESERVED

■ MASTERWORKS

William H. Winslow House
River Forest, Illinois, 1893–1894
Perspective (detail). Ink on tracing paper, 16¼ x 23⅛ in.
9305.001

BOX 6099　ROHNERT PARK　CA 94927

Pomegranate

© THE FRANK LLOYD WRIGHT FOUNDATION
TALIESIN WEST, SCOTTSDALE, ARIZONA. ALL RIGHTS RESERVED

■ MASTERWORKS

Larkin Company Administration Building
Buffalo, New York, 1902–1906
Perspective. Pencil on tracing paper, 24 x 14 in.
0403.001

Pomegranate · BOX 6099 ROHNERT PARK CA 94927

© THE FRANK LLOYD WRIGHT FOUNDATION
TALIESIN WEST, SCOTTSDALE, ARIZONA. ALL RIGHTS RESERVED

■ MASTERWORKS

Susan Lawrence Dana House
Springfield, Illinois, 1902–1904
Interior perspective: dining room. Pencil and watercolor on paper, 25 x 20⅜ in.
Erving and Joyce Wolf Collection 9905.003

Pomegranate

BOX 6099 ROHNERT PARK CA 94927

FRANK LLOYD WRIGHT COLLECTION
© THE FRANK LLOYD WRIGHT FOUNDATION
TALIESIN WEST, SCOTTSDALE, ARIZONA. ALL RIGHTS RESERVED

■ MASTERWORKS

K. C. DeRhodes House
South Bend, Indiana, 1906.
Perspective. Pencil, ink, and watercolor on paper, 18¾ x 25¾ in.
0602.001

BOX 6099   ROHNERT PARK   CA 94927

Pomegranate

FRANK LLOYD WRIGHT® COLLECTION
© THE FRANK LLOYD WRIGHT FOUNDATION
TALIESIN WEST, SCOTTSDALE, ARIZONA. ALL RIGHTS RESERVED

■ MASTERWORKS

"Wingspread" (Herbert F. Johnson House)
Racine, Wisconsin. 1937–1939
Perspective. Pencil and color pencil on tracing paper, 16⅞ x 40 in.
3703.002

Pomegranate   BOX 6099   ROHNERT PARK   CA 94927

FRANK LLOYD WRIGHT® COLLECTION
© THE FRANK LLOYD WRIGHT FOUNDATION
TALIESIN WEST, SCOTTSDALE, ARIZONA. ALL RIGHTS RESERVED

■ MASTERWORKS

John C. Pew House
Madison, Wisconsin, 1938–1940
Perspective. Pencil and color pencil on tracing paper, 22 x 36 in.
4012.002

Pomegranate BOX 6099 ROHNERT PARK CA 94927

FRANK LLOYD WRIGHT® COLLECTION © THE FRANK LLOYD WRIGHT FOUNDATION
TALIESIN WEST, SCOTTSDALE, ARIZONA. ALL RIGHTS RESERVED

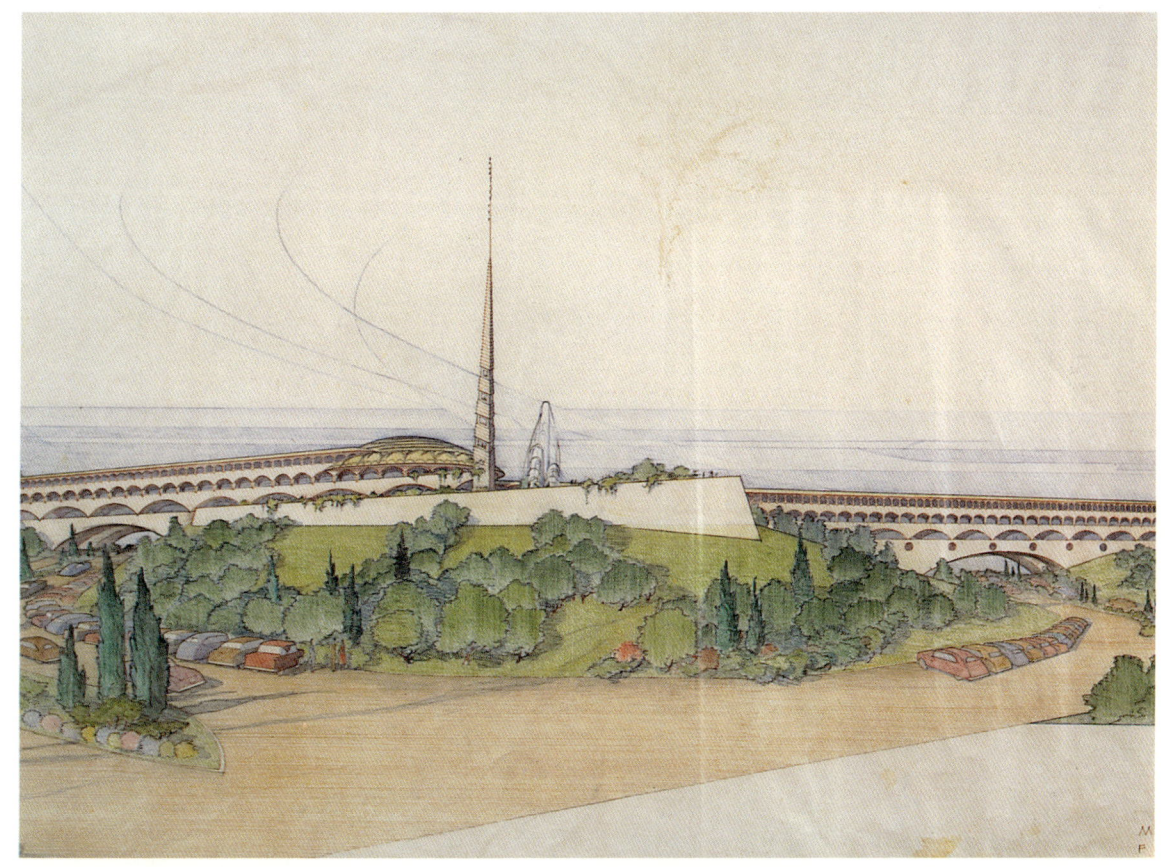

■ MASTERWORKS

Marin County Civic Center
San Rafael, California, 1957–1962
Perspective. Crayon and ink on tracing paper, 34 x 83 in.
5746.015

Pomegranate BOX 6099 ROHNERT PARK CA 94927

FRANK LLOYD WRIGHT COLLECTION
© THE FRANK LLOYD WRIGHT FOUNDATION
TALIESIN WEST, SCOTTSDALE, ARIZONA. ALL RIGHTS RESERVED

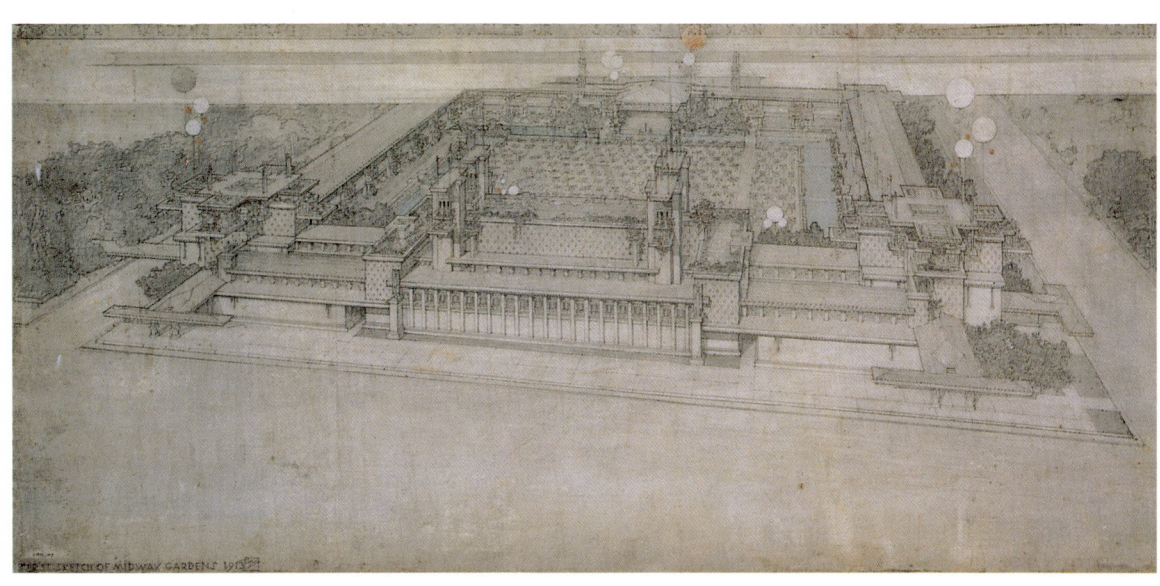

■ MASTERWORKS

Midway Gardens
Chicago, Illinois, 1913–1914 (demolished 1929)
Perspective. Pencil, ink, and ink wash on linen, 16⅝ x 40⅝ in.
1401.007

Pomegranate   BOX 6099   ROHNERT PARK   CA 94927

© THE FRANK LLOYD WRIGHT FOUNDATION
TALIESIN WEST, SCOTTSDALE, ARIZONA. ALL RIGHTS RESERVED

FRANK LLOYD WRIGHT® COLLECTION

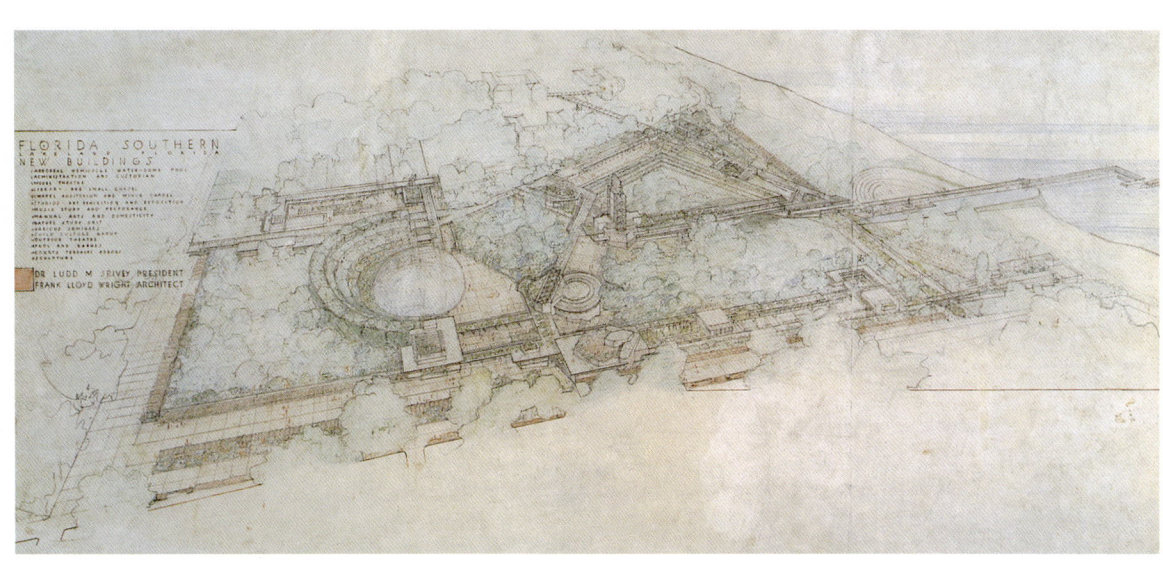

◼ MASTERWORKS

Florida Southern College
Lakeland, Florida, begun 1938
Aerial perspective. Pencil and color pencil on tracing paper,
24¼ x 48 in.
3805.002

Pomegranate BOX 6099 ROHNERT PARK CA 94927

© THE FRANK LLOYD WRIGHT FOUNDATION
TALIESIN WEST, SCOTTSDALE, ARIZONA. ALL RIGHTS RESERVED

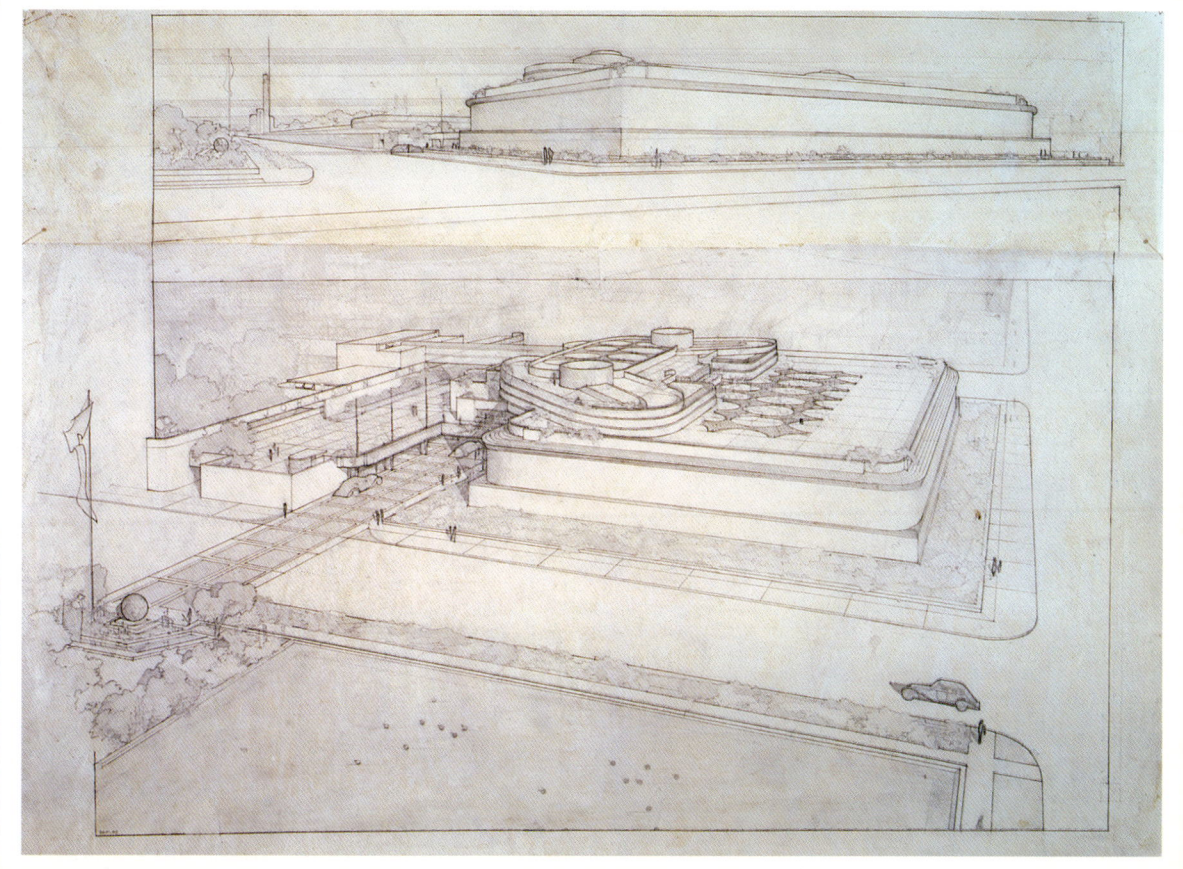

■ MASTERWORKS

S. C. Johnson & Son, Inc. Administration Building
Racine, Wisconsin, 1936–1939
Perspectives. Pencil, color pencil, and ink on tracing paper,
28¾ x 38⅝ in.
3601.002/003

BOX 6099 ROHNERT PARK CA 94927

Pomegranate

FRANK LLOYD WRIGHT COLLECTION
© THE FRANK LLOYD WRIGHT FOUNDATION
TALIESIN WEST, SCOTTSDALE, ARIZONA. ALL RIGHTS RESERVED

■ MASTERWORKS

"La Miniatura" (Mrs. George Madison Millard House)
Pasadena, California, 1923
Perspective. Color pencil and pencil on paper, 9¾ x 13¾ in.
2302.001

Pomegranate   BOX 6099   ROHNERT PARK   CA 94927

FRANK LLOYD WRIGHT COLLECTION
© THE FRANK LLOYD WRIGHT FOUNDATION
TALIESIN WEST, SCOTTSDALE, ARIZONA. ALL RIGHTS RESERVED

■ MASTERWORKS

Frank Lloyd Wright Home and Studio
Oak Park, Illinois, 1889–1898
Perspective. Sepia ink on paper, 6¼ x 19⅝ in.
9506.001

Pomegranate BOX 6099 ROHNERT PARK CA 94927

© THE FRANK LLOYD WRIGHT FOUNDATION
TALIESIN WEST, SCOTTSDALE, ARIZONA. ALL RIGHTS RESERVED

■ MASTERWORKS

Ward W. Willits House
Highland Park, Illinois, 1902–1903
Perspective. Crayon, gouache, ink, and ink wash on paper,
8½ x 32 in.
0208.001

Pomegranate   BOX 6099   ROHNERT PARK   CA 94927

 © THE FRANK LLOYD WRIGHT FOUNDATION
TALIESIN WEST, SCOTTSDALE, ARIZONA. ALL RIGHTS RESERVED

■MASTERWORKS

Solomon R. Guggenheim Museum
New York, New York, 1943–1959
Perspective. Color pencil, pencil, and ink on tracing paper,
26 x 39½ in.
4305.017

Pomegranate BOX 6099 ROHNERT PARK CA 94927

FRANK LLOYD WRIGHT® COLLECTION © THE FRANK LLOYD WRIGHT FOUNDATION TALIESIN WEST, SCOTTSDALE, ARIZONA. ALL RIGHTS RESERVED

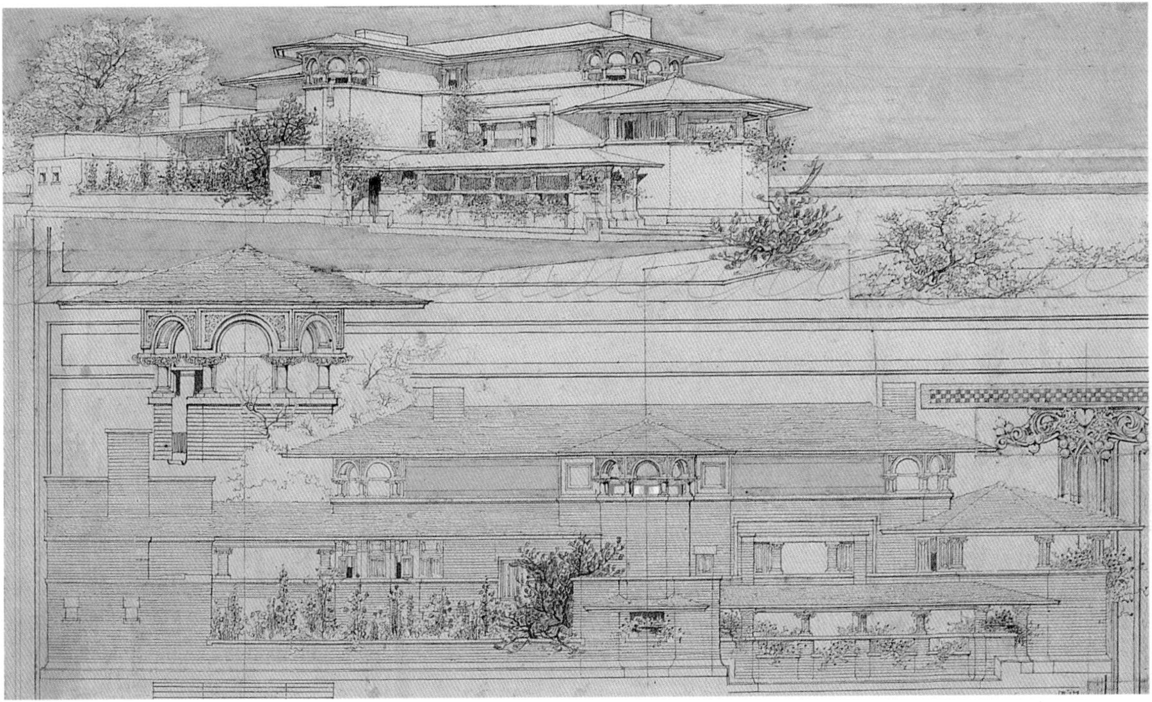

■ MASTERWORKS

Joseph Husser House
Chicago, Illinois, 1899 (demolished c. 1923–1924)
Perspective and elevation. Ink and ink wash on paper, 17 x 23 in.
Erving and Joyce Wolf Collection 9901.001

Pomegranate   BOX 6099   ROHNERT PARK   CA 94927

FRANK LLOYD WRIGHT COLLECTION © THE FRANK LLOYD WRIGHT FOUNDATION TALIESIN WEST, SCOTTSDALE, ARIZONA. ALL RIGHTS RESERVED

1906

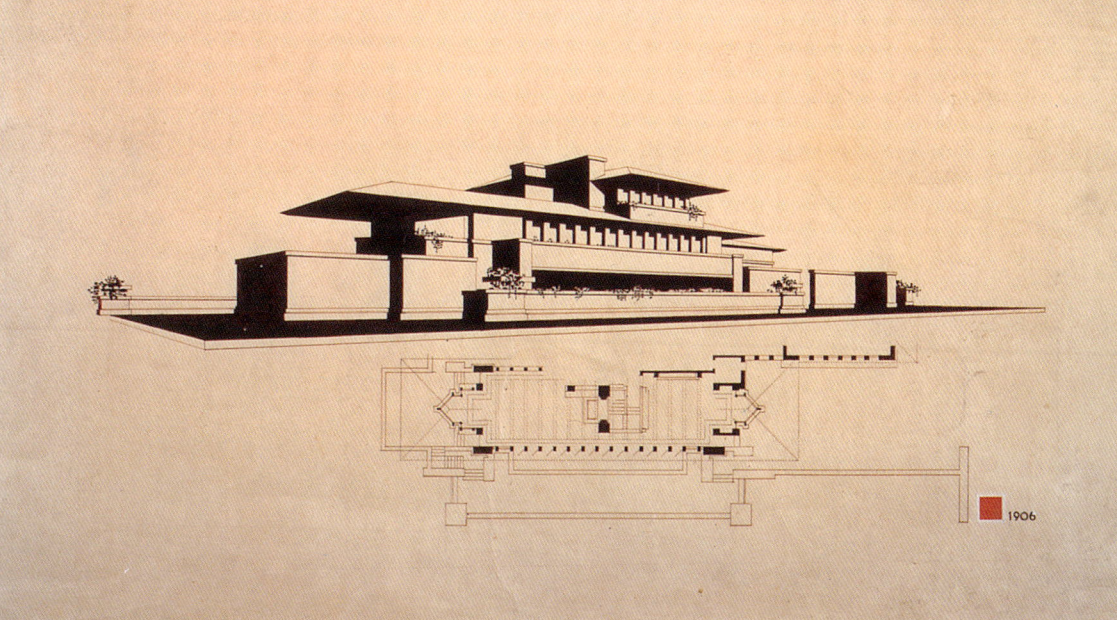

■ MASTERWORKS

Frederick C. Robie House
Chicago, Illinois, 1908–1910
Perspective and first-floor plan. Ink on paper, 21½ x 37½ in.
Erving and Joyce Wolf Collection 0908.003

Pomegranate   BOX 6099   ROHNERT PARK   CA 94927

© THE FRANK LLOYD WRIGHT FOUNDATION
TALIESIN WEST, SCOTTSDALE, ARIZONA. ALL RIGHTS RESERVED

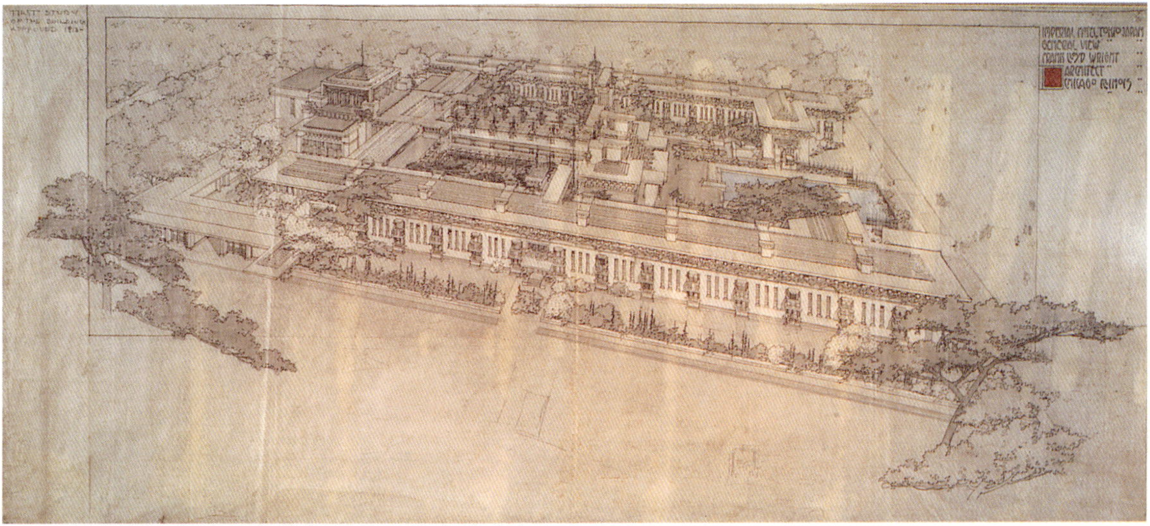
IMPERIAL HOTEL TOKYO JAPAN
GENERAL VIEW
FRANK LLOYD WRIGHT
ARCHITECT
CHICAGO ILLINOIS

■ masterworks

Imperial Hotel
Tokyo, Japan, c. 1912–1923 (demolished 1968)
First scheme. Aerial perspective. Pencil, color pencil, and ink on linen, 33½ x 74½ in.

Erving and Joyce Wolf Collection 1509.003

Pomegranate BOX 6099 ROHNERT PARK CA 94927

FRANK LLOYD WRIGHT® COLLECTION © THE FRANK LLOYD WRIGHT FOUNDATION TALIESIN WEST, SCOTTSDALE, ARIZONA. ALL RIGHTS RESERVED

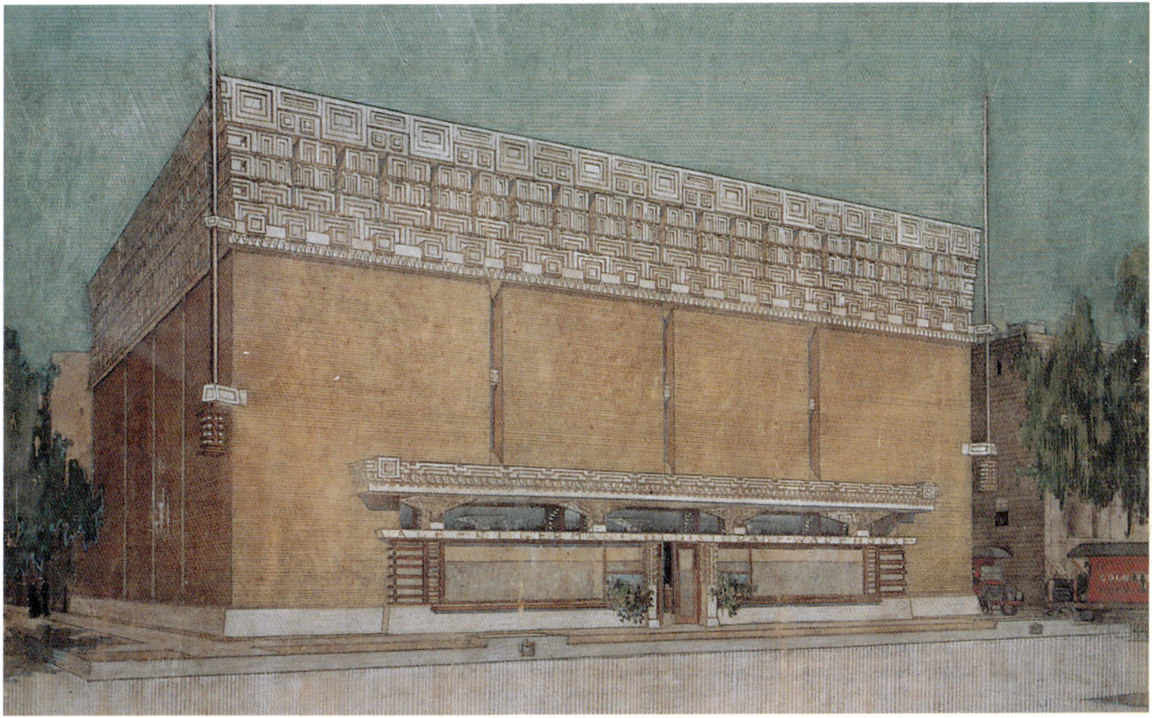

■ MASTERWORKS

A. D. German Warehouse
Richland Center, Wisconsin, 1915–1920
Perspective. Pencil, pastel, and gouache on paper and linen,
21½ x 24⅜ in.

Erving and Joyce Wolf Collection 1504.001

Pomegranate   BOX 6099   ROHNERT PARK   CA 94927

FRANK LLOYD WRIGHT® COLLECTION © THE FRANK LLOYD WRIGHT FOUNDATION TALIESIN WEST, SCOTTSDALE, ARIZONA. ALL RIGHTS RESERVED

MR. C. THAXTER SHAW
RESIDENCE · MONTREAL
DINING ROOM
FRANK LLOYD WRIGHT
ARCHITECT
OAK PARK · ILLINOIS

■ MASTERWORKS

C. Thaxter Shaw House
Montreal, Quebec, Canada, 1906
Interior perspective. Ink, pencil, and watercolor on tracing paper,
7⅝ x 15⅜ in.
0610.007

Pomegranate   BOX 6099   ROHNERT PARK CA 94927

FRANK LLOYD WRIGHT COLLECTION © THE FRANK LLOYD WRIGHT FOUNDATION TALIESIN WEST, SCOTTSDALE, ARIZONA. ALL RIGHTS RESERVED

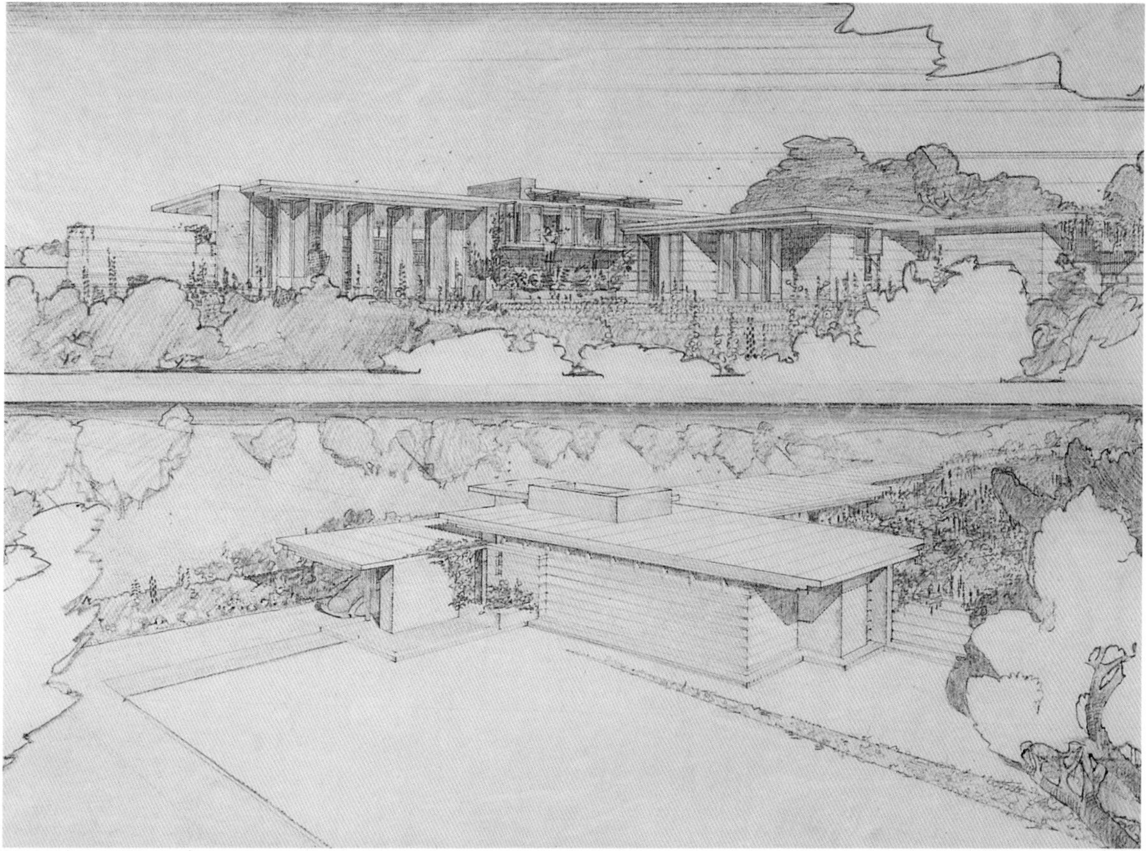

■masterworks

Herbert Jacobs House
Madison, Wisconsin, 1936–1937
Perspective and aerial perspective. Pencil, color pencil, and ink on tracing paper, 21 x 31¾ in.
3702.002/003

Pomegranate BOX 6099 ROHNERT PARK CA 94927

FRANK LLOYD WRIGHT® COLLECTION © THE FRANK LLOYD WRIGHT FOUNDATION TALIESIN WEST, SCOTTSDALE, ARIZONA. ALL RIGHTS RESERVED

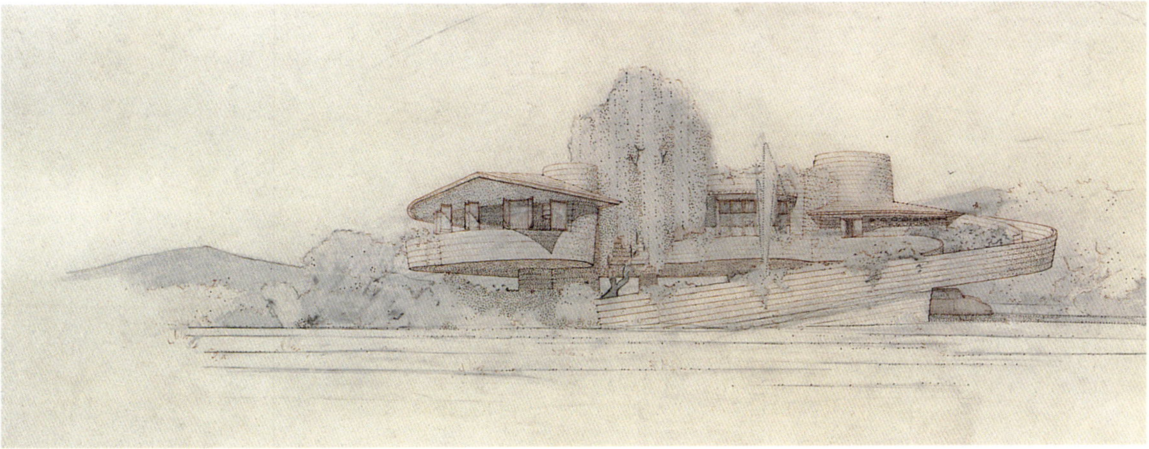

■ MASTERWORKS

David Wright House
Phoenix, Arizona, 1950–1952
Perspective. Pencil on tracing paper, 28 x 36 in.
5011.002

Pomegranate BOX 6099 ROHNERT PARK CA 94927

FRANK LLOYD WRIGHT COLLECTION © THE FRANK LLOYD WRIGHT FOUNDATION
TALIESIN WEST, SCOTTSDALE, ARIZONA. ALL RIGHTS RESERVED

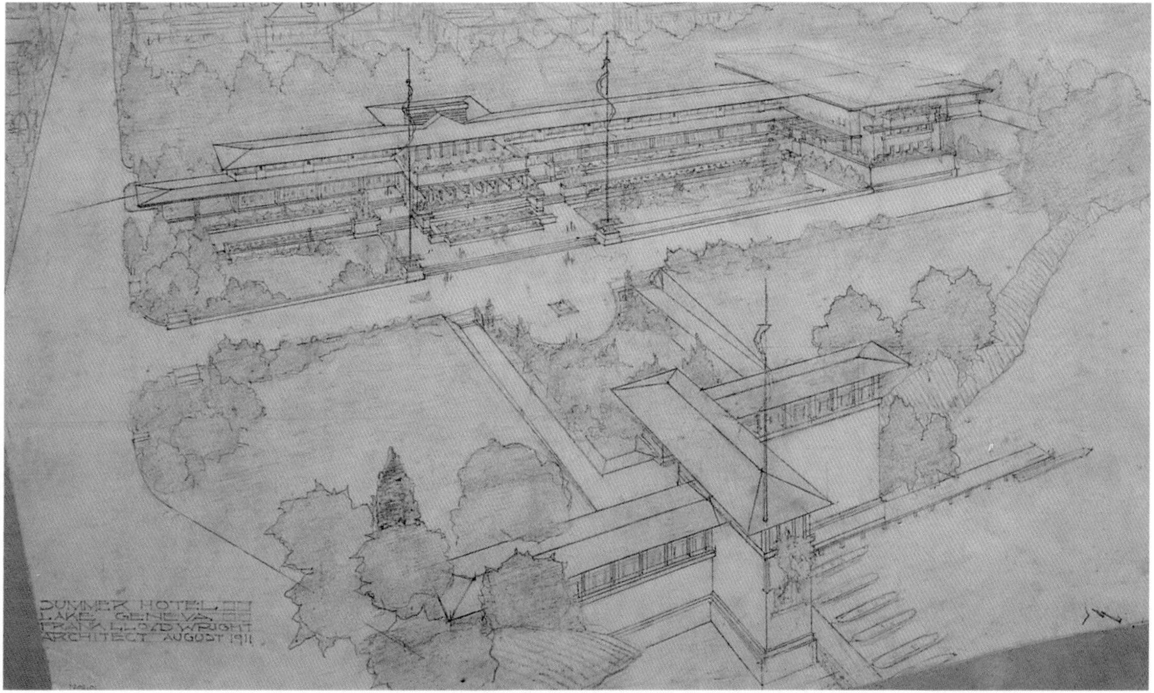
SUMMER HOTEL
LAKE GENEVA
FRANK LLOYD WRIGHT
ARCHITECT AUGUST 1911

■ MASTERWORKS

Lake Geneva Inn
Lake Geneva, Wisconsin, 1911 (demolished 1970)
Aerial perspective. Pencil and color pencil on tracing paper, 23¼ x 13½ in.
1202.001

Pomegranate   BOX 6099   ROHNERT PARK   CA 94927

FRANK LLOYD WRIGHT® COLLECTION
© THE FRANK LLOYD WRIGHT FOUNDATION
TALIESIN WEST, SCOTTSDALE, ARIZONA. ALL RIGHTS RESERVED

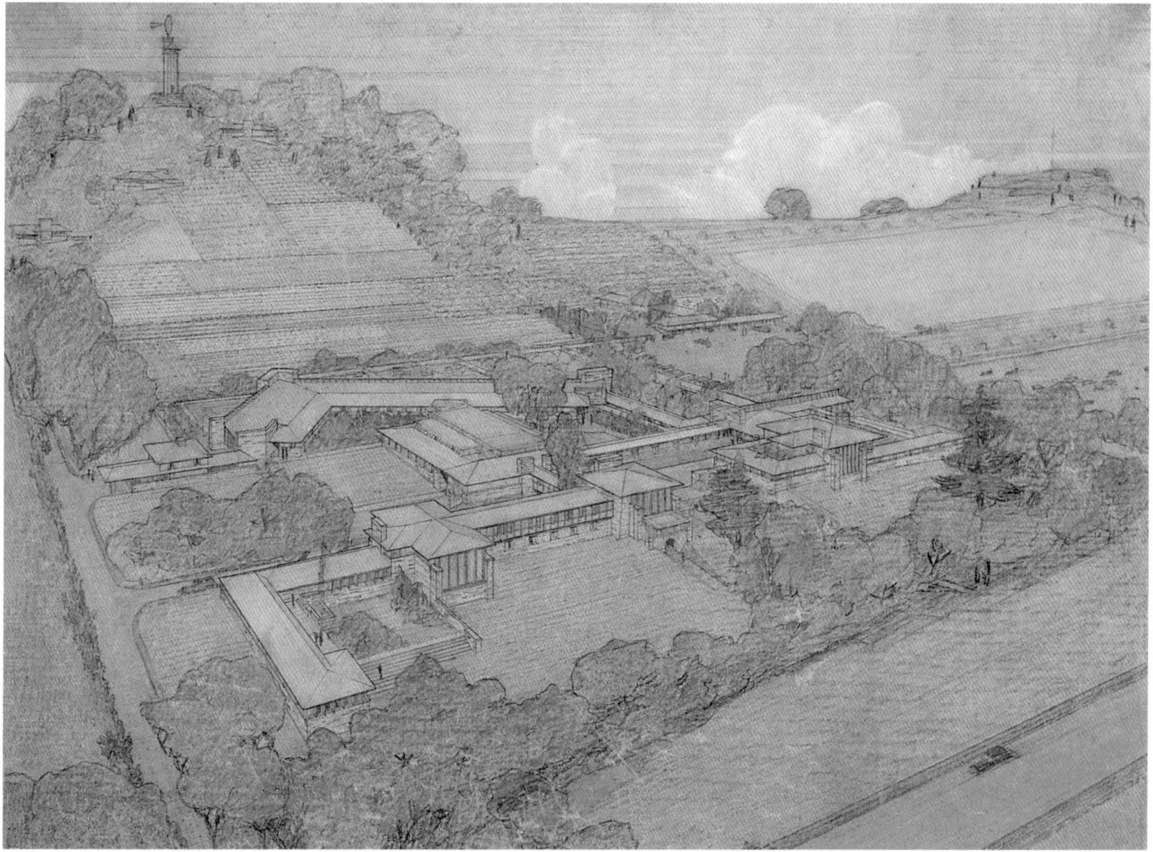

■ MASTERWORKS

Taliesin Fellowship Complex
Spring Green, Wisconsin, 1932
Aerial Perspective. Pencil and color pencil on tracing paper.
17¼ x 20½ in.
3301.001

Pomegranate   BOX 6099   ROHNERT PARK   CA 94927

FRANK LLOYD WRIGHT® COLLECTION
© THE FRANK LLOYD WRIGHT FOUNDATION
TALIESIN WEST, SCOTTSDALE, ARIZONA. ALL RIGHTS RESERVED

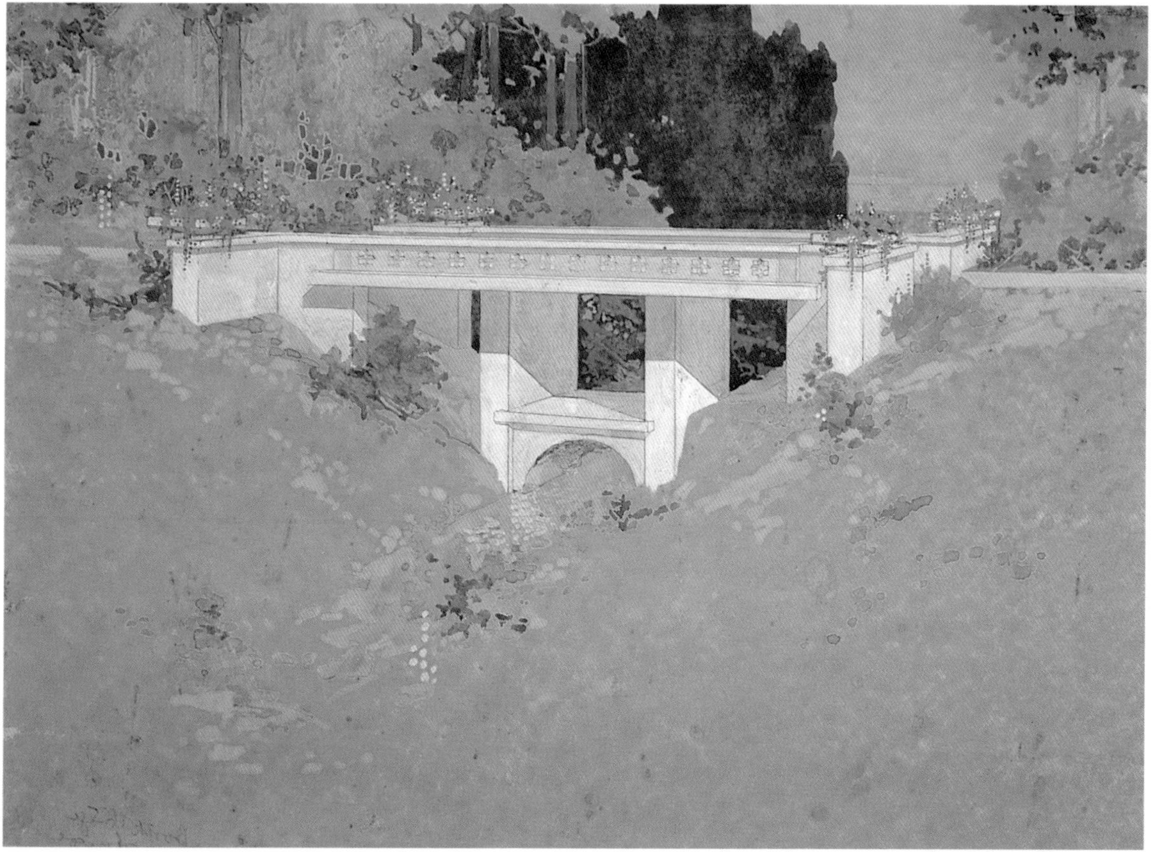

■ MASTERWORKS

Ravine Bluffs Bridge
Glencoe, Illinois, 1915
Perspective. Watercolor and watercolor wash on art paper,
24 x 18 in.
1505.001

Pomegranate BOX 6099 ROHNERT PARK CA 94927

© THE FRANK LLOYD WRIGHT FOUNDATION
TALIESIN WEST, SCOTTSDALE, ARIZONA. ALL RIGHTS RESERVED

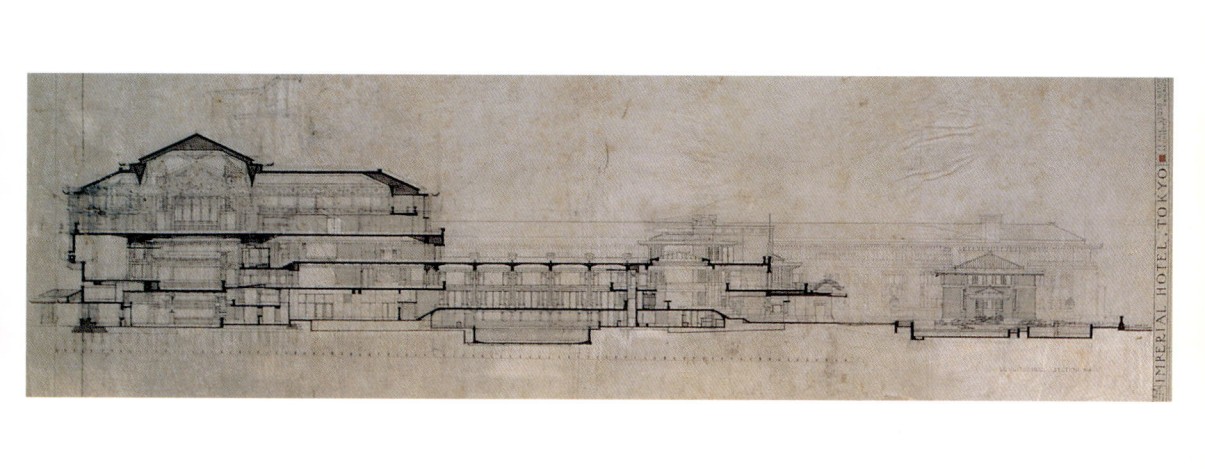

IMPERIAL HOTEL, TOKYO

■ MASTERWORKS

Imperial Hotel
Tokyo, Japan, 1912–1923 (demolished 1968)
Longitudinal section. Ink, ink wash, and pencil on linen,
20 ⅛ x 60 ⅝ in.
1509.650

Pomegranate   BOX 6099   ROHNERT PARK   CA 94927

FRANK LLOYD WRIGHT® COLLECTION
© THE FRANK LLOYD WRIGHT FOUNDATION
TALIESIN WEST, SCOTTSDALE, ARIZONA. ALL RIGHTS RESERVED

EXTENSION AND TERMINAL OF MONONA AVENUE
SEVEN ACRES OF MADE OVER EXISTING RAILROAD TRACKS — FLOOR PARKING
LAKE WATER THROWN UP INTO MONUMENTAL FOUNTAINS   MONONA AVE.   "THE CITY GOES TO THE LAKE"   SEVEN MONTHS WATERDOMES, FIVE MONTHS EVERGREENS INSTEAD
CIVIC AUDITORIUM SEATING 10,000, FRONTING OLIN TERRACE
COUNTY JAIL AND OFFICES, CITY HALL, UNION RAILROAD DEPOT.   COST $17,500,000. RAISED BY —?   (SEE KAUFMANN & CO PITTSBURGH)

■MASTERWORKS

Monona Terrace Civic Center
Madison, Wisconsin, 1938–1953
Aerial perspective. Pencil, color pencil, and ink on tracing paper, 17 ¼ x 40 in.
3909.002

Pomegranate BOX 6099 ROHNERT PARK CA 94927

FRANK LLOYD WRIGHT® COLLECTION
© THE FRANK LLOYD WRIGHT FOUNDATION
TALIESIN WEST, SCOTTSDALE, ARIZONA. ALL RIGHTS RESERVED

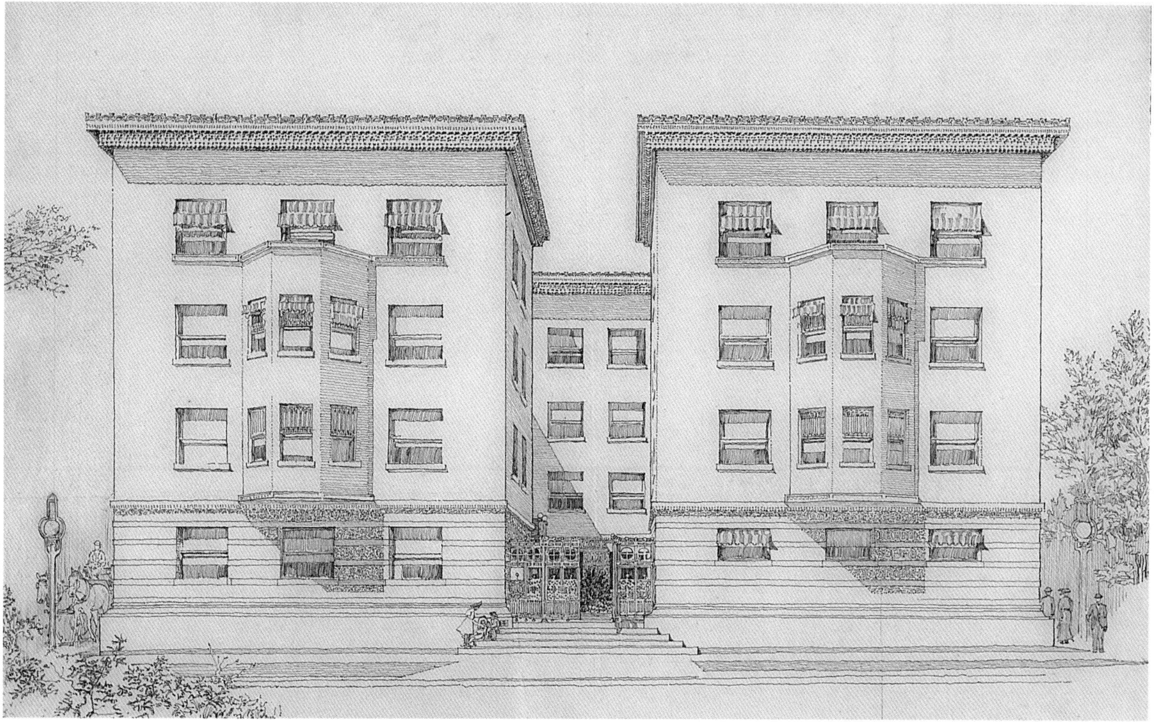

■ MASTERWORKS

Francis Apartments
Chicago, Illinois, 1895 (demolished 1971)
Perspective. Ink on tracing paper, 14⅜ x 24⅛ in.
9501.001

Pomegranate   BOX 6099   ROHNERT PARK   CA 94927

FRANK LLOYD WRIGHT® COLLECTION © THE FRANK LLOYD WRIGHT FOUNDATION TALIESIN WEST, SCOTTSDALE, ARIZONA. ALL RIGHTS RESERVED

■MASTERWORKS

Charles E. Ennis House
Los Angeles, California 1923–1924
Perspective and partial plan Pencil, color pencil, and ink on tracing paper, 20¼ x 39 in.
2401.003

Pomegranate BOX 6099 ROHNERT PARK CA 94927

FRANK LLOYD WRIGHT COLLECTION® © THE FRANK LLOYD WRIGHT FOUNDATION TALIESIN WEST, SCOTTSDALE, ARIZONA. ALL RIGHTS RESERVED